The amazing story of . . .

# Jesus in Worship & Wonder

## Melody, Mystery & The Messiah

Psalms 1–150

# 10

The amazing story of . . .

# Jesus in Worship
# & Wonder

Melody, Mystery
& The Messiah

## Psalms 1–150

Let the word of Christ dwell in you richly; in all wisdom
teaching and cheering each other on with psalms,
hymns, and spiritual songs, singing with grace in your
heart to the Lord. **Colossians 3:16**

Because what we worship we become like!

Published by PUSH Publishing 2018

www.pushpublishing.co.uk

in partnership with Jesus Centred Bible

office@jesuscentred.org

www.jesuscentred.org

Copyright © Christen Forster, 2018

All rights reserved. No part of this publication may be
reproduced, stored in a retrieval system, or transmitted
in any form or by means, electronic, mechanical,
photocopying or otherwise, without the prior written
consent of the publisher. Short extracts may be used for
review purposes.

Scripture quotations are based on the World English
Bible (WEB) which is in the public domain.
The WEB is a 1997 revision of the American Standard
Version of 1901.

A catalogue record for this book is
available from the British Library

ISBN-13: 978-0-9933445-9-6

Printed and bound in Great Britain by Cambrian Printers

Cover design by Joseph Laycock

# Contents

# Dedication

Special thanks to:

All those who enable me to write these books, by their support and partnership. In particular I would like to mention . . .

Beryl Berrett, Jean Berrill, Paul Blakeman, Grant Bones, Mary Brown, Shelagh Foster, Serenia France, Lucy Freckleton, Martin and Rachel Hall, Derek and Angie King, Richard and Ruth Mackay, Sharon McIlroy, Mark Picken and Flavia Yousef.

Without you, these books would not get written.

# Introduction

Jesus said:

> ' . . . all things which were written about Me in the Law of Moses, the Prophets, and the Psalms must be fulfilled'. Then He opened their minds so they could understand the Scriptures. **Luke 24:44–45**

Jesus has previously claimed that the Scriptures were all about Him (see **John 5:39** and **Luke 24:27**) but, on this final occasion, Jesus explicitly mentions the **Psalms** as He opens His disciples' minds to *understand* more than there would ever be time to teach them.

Jesus quotes from **Psalms** more often than from any other book of the Old Testament. This might not be a surprise given that it is the longest book in the Bible but the **Psalms** clearly informed Jesus' ministry and mission. As worship, they defined the culture that formed Jesus' humanity. They taught Jesus how to engage Heaven into the pains and joys of everyday life. Jesus would have read, recited and sung every **Psalm** many times over as He grew in wisdom, stature and favour, **Luke 2:52**.

1

Exactly half of the **Psalms** are ascribed in some way to David, 73 include 'of David' in their title and **Psalms 2** and **91** are attributed to David in the New Testament (**Acts 4:25** and **Hebrews 4:7**). So 75 out of 150 **Psalms** belong to David, but that doesn't necessarily mean that David wrote them all. The phrase 'of David' could simply mean a **Psalm** was composed as part of the worship overseen by David.

David's tabernacle was producing worship for 40 years alongside the tabernacle of Moses until both were replaced by Solomon's Temple. In Hebrew, the phrase 'of David' is *l-dud* / לדוד which more broadly means 'to / for David'. And 'David' / דוד simply means 'beloved'. It is the word for a cherished family member; brides, grooms, uncles and sisters are all called 'beloved'.

So half of the **Psalms** are addressed 'to / for a beloved one', for God's people generally and for the 'beloved son' specifically. They instruct and inspire us as beloved family just as they did Jesus, the beloved Son.

Now, there is not the space in this book to consider all 150 **Psalms** but we can learn from the ones we do explore. Like the disciples at the end of Luke we have examples to learn from, the events of the Gospels, and the guidance of the Holy Spirit to safely open our minds to understand God's words for ourselves.

Discovering the historic Jesus in the pages that prepared the world for His coming is a foundation of the fruitful Christian life. Study becomes worship when we see and are thrilled by discovering Him. You will get the most out of this book if you set your heart to worship alongside a mind to learn. I understand the **Psalms** best when I read them with the same awe that inspired them.

Knowing facts puffs us up, seeing Jesus changes us.

Using these notes

The table on page 5 lists all seven streams of revelation used in this series to show how Jesus is presented in the Old Testament. Each stream appears in the book of **Psalms.**

**Now Psalms** is rich with prophetic content; it is peppered with ethical and theological ideas found in Jesus' teaching, and it uses typological titles and images too. **Psalms** has a lot to say about the 'Messiah', but Christophanies are thin on the ground.

So this book is arranged into three broadly themed *Parts* and an *Appendix*.

   *Part 1* looks at the **Psalms** which use the typological

title 'Messiah'. These **Psalms** are all prophetic in some way as they all anticipate the Messiah who is to come while also looking back at David, the prototype Messiah and a key figure in Jesus' family tree.

*Part 2* looks at prophecy in the **Psalms** and is grouped by the three sub-streams which we have previously identified and worked with: Predictive, Ecstatic and Formative Prophecy.

*Part 3* explores Types, Teaching and the Trinity in **Psalms**.

*The Appendix* contains a numerical list of all the **Psalms** covered in this book, with associated page references for those who would rather work through the **Psalms** in the order they appear in the Bible.

Whichever way you read the material, you will gain the most long-term benefit if you take time to transfer the information into a study Bible. It will help too to have a Bible to hand to read each **Psalm** as we study it, (constraints on space have required us to be efficient with our words).

Annotating your Bible is a good thing. I've found my own love and understanding of Scripture has grown as I rediscover notes years after I've added and forgotten them. In time, notes become your revelation much more than just learned information!

To aid this process, you can use different coloured pencils to mark the different revelation streams, and each has an icon that can be drawn in your Bible if you don't have a coloured pencil to hand. Finally, you'll notice I regularly include Strong's reference numbers in brackets to encourage further study!

So, let's get started!

 **Prophecy:** Predictive, Ecstatic and Formative

 **Typology:** Models, Titles, People and Events

 **Teaching:** Used by Jesus / Gospels

 **Jesus' Household:** The Family Tree

 **Trinity and Divinity:** Jesus as God / God as a Plurality

 **Christophanies:** God in visible form

 **Cryptic:** Hidden in the Hebrew

# Part 1

## Messianic Psalms

# The Messianic Psalms

There are eight **Psalms** that use the title 'Messiah' / משיח (#H4899). For the Rabbis in the century before Jesus, these **Psalms** were part of the debate and discussion about their coming Saviour.

We are going to consider them together. They are very important in understanding the 'type' of role that Jesus fulfilled.

In fact, over half of the first *Messianic Psalm* is quoted directly or indirectly in the New Testament.

##  Psalm 2 – My Son the Messiah

**Psalm 2** is based on the experiences of David, but it looks beyond him to a time when the world would acknowledge *YHWH*'s Messiah, 'the Son'. It is both predictive and formative, anticipating Jesus while guiding and shaping Him too. It ends with a victorious Son, having started with an opposed Messiah.

Why do the Gentiles mob together and the peoples plot a vain thing? The kings of the earth take a stand, and the rulers take counsel together against *YHWH*, and against His **Anointed-Messiah. Psalm 2:1–2**

These words are quoted in **Acts 4:25–26** as the Church experiences opposition for the first time. The Church spells out exactly who was involved in this opposition: '. . . against your **holy servant Jesus, whom you anointed**, both Herod [a **king of the earth**] and Pontius Pilate [a ruler], with the Gentiles and the people of Israel, were gathered together . . . ', **Acts 4:27**.

And in the week that Jesus was crucified, Matthew quotes them too, word-for-word as they appear in the Septuagint (the Greek version of the Old Testament):

They [the rulers] **gathered themselves together** / συνηχθησαν επι το αυτο. **Matthew 22:34**

. . . against Jesus, just as **Psalm 2** describes:

The rulers **take counsel together** / συνηχθησαν επι το αυτο . . . against *YHWH* and His Messiah. **Psalm 2:2b (Septuagint)**

From its beginning, the Church knew that **Psalm 2** was a prediction of Jesus the Christ.

**Psalm 2** goes on to say that *YHWH* is not impressed with this widespread opposition to His Messiah, but God simply laughs and says:

> I have installed my King on Zion my Holy Mountain. **Psalm 2:6**.

Now, the Hebrew word translated here as 'installed', is *nawsak* / נסך (#H5258) which is usually translated as 'poured out', 'poured over' or 'poured onto'. It was how a drink offering was given as sacrifice (see **Numbers 28:7**). Once oil had been 'poured onto' a king or priest they were commissioned in their position, so our English Bibles say 'installed' or 'set in place'. The 'pouring onto' is the anointing that sets the Messiah in His role.

At Jesus' Baptism, the waters of the Jordan poured over Him and, as He came out of the water, the Holy Spirit poured onto Him. Then Jesus hears the words:

> You are My Son, beloved, with whom I am well pleased. **Matthew 3:17b**

This commission is made up of three parts, each of which spoke to the nature of Jesus' Messiahship. Jesus would have meditated on the Old Testament passages each part had been drawn from as He left the Jordan to pray and fast for direction in the wilderness, **Matthew 4:1–11**.

- 'My Son' was recognised as a title for the Messiah in the Rabbinic writings and teachings of Jesus' day because of **Psalm 2**. In it the Messiah declares:

   I will tell of the decree: *YHWH* said to me, 'You are my Son; today I have confirmed (begotten or acquired) you.' **Psalm 2:7**

- 'Beloved' is the title of the bridegroom in the **Song of Solomon** and Jesus applied the title 'the Bridegroom' to Himself from the very beginning of His public ministry.

- 'With whom I am well pleased' is a quote from **Isaiah** referencing the Suffering Servant and Jesus understood suffering as a part of His commission.

The decree of sonship marks the beginning of Jesus' ministry as the Christ, but His Baptism is not the only anointing event in His life.

The New Testament also recognises an anointing at Jesus' Baptism (**Mark 1:9–12**), His death (**Mark 14:3**), and His ascension (**Hebrews 1:9** quoting **Psalm 45**, see page 39). Interestingly David was anointed three times too; first with his family (**1 Samuel 16:13**), then by the tribe of Judah (**2 Samuel 2:4**) and finally by the whole nation of Israel (**2 Samuel 5:3**).

In the wonderfully multilayered way which prophecy works, **Psalm 2** is both quoted and illuminated by all three of Jesus' anointing events.

## 1. Baptism

Jesus' Baptism reflected a rite found in many of the world's classical cultures, that of formally 'adopting' or installing an heir.

Paul draws on these 'adoption' rituals to illustrate our growth into Christian maturity, **Romans 8:15–30**. In the Roman world, the rite was commonly associated with the heirs of the powerful entering the Senate. A nobleman would take his chosen heir to a public place, like the steps of the Forum, he would make a public declaration and promises over the son, and give him a symbolic gift as a sign of his new authority.

All these elements are present at Jesus' Baptism. There is a declaration and a gift, the promise is implicit from **Psalm 2**, which follows the declaration with:

> Ask of Me, and I will surely give you the Gentiles
> / nations as your inheritance, and the ends of
> the earth as your possession. **Psalm 2:8**

Jesus carried this promise of the 'nations' into the wilderness where it became a point of contention with the devil:

> The devil . . . showed Him all the kingdoms of
> the world, and . . . said to Him, 'I will give you all
> of these things, if you will fall down and worship
> me.' **Matthew 4:9**

The devil offers Jesus an easier path to 'the nations' than the opposition described in **Psalm 2**.

 Jesus resists the temptation and chooses the route of the Suffering Servant in whom YHWH is well pleased. He starts His public preaching with the anointing verses for the Suffering Servant.

> The Spirit of the Lord is upon me . . .
> **Luke 4:18** and **Isaiah 61:1**

Following His suffering, death and resurrection Jesus involves us in claiming His inheritance, 'the ends of the earth'. Jesus' last instruction at His ascension was: '. . . and you will be my witnesses . . . to the farthest parts of the earth', **Acts 1:8**.

Now, Jesus' Baptism happened in the Jordan valley to the east of Jerusalem, but **Psalm 2** locates the Messiah's installation on 'Zion my Holy Mountain', **Psalm 2:6**. There is clearly an element of **Psalm 2** that was not completed at Jesus' Baptism, but His death, resurrection and ascension did happen on hills in and next to Jerusalem.

 2. Crucifixion

 We have noted that Matthew quotes **Psalm 2** during Jesus' Crucifixion week. In fact on the same day that the 'rulers take counsel together' against Jesus, Jesus was anointed for a second time. That evening Mary anointed Jesus in

Bethany. She uses nard, a costly perfume oil, **John 12:3–8**, and Jesus accepts Mary's extravagance: 'She has anointed My body beforehand for burial,' **Mark 14:8**.

 Jesus knows that His anointing is that of the Suffering Servant, but the watching crowds understood it differently. Just two days earlier they had seen Jesus ride into Jerusalem on a donkey. Jesus was the anointed Messiah-King of **Zechariah 9:9** and Mary's act confirmed this to them.

The following day, Jesus had to address this tension again as He ate the Last Supper with His disciples. They were debating how many swords they needed, so Jesus explained the pain of His impending Passion using the imagery of the drink offering:

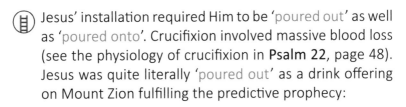

> This is My blood . . . poured out for many . . .
> **Matthew 26:28, Mark 14:24**

 Jesus' installation required Him to be 'poured out' as well as 'poured onto'. Crucifixion involved massive blood loss (see the physiology of crucifixion in **Psalm 22, page 48**). Jesus was quite literally 'poured out' as a drink offering on Mount Zion fulfilling the predictive prophecy:

> I have installed / poured onto / poured out (nawsak / נסך) my King on Zion my Holy Mountain. **Psalm 2:6**

Jesus' second anointing started with Him being 'poured

onto' in the hills outside Jerusalem and ended with Him being 'poured out' on the slopes of the Temple Mount as predicted in **Psalm 2**.

In the New Testament we find an understanding that Jesus' Baptism anticipated the Cross. Going down into the waters was symbolic of death, coming up was symbolic of resurrection (see **Romans 6:4**, **Colossians 2:12**). Resurrection was the first step in Jesus' ascension to the Father's right hand, where we read about Jesus' third anointing.

 3. Ascension

Paul quotes **Psalm 2:7** on his first missionary journey, referring to Jesus' resurrection and ascension.

> God . . . raised up Jesus. As it is also written in the **second Psalm**, 'You are my Son, today I have begotten you'. **Acts 13:33**

But it is **Hebrews** that firmly connects **Psalm 2** with the anointing that happened with Jesus' ascension. Using the same quote that Paul used in Pisidian Antioch, the writer of the book of **Hebrews** (whom I suspect was Lucius of Cyrene, Paul's mentor, better known to us as Luke the Gospel writer) opens his book with **Psalm 2**:

> For to which of the angels did God ever say, 'You are my Son, today I have begotten you?' . . . 'God, has anointed you with the oil of gladness above your fellows.' **Hebrew 1:5, 9**

Towards the end of **Hebrews** we discover that, 'Jesus . . . for the joy set before Him endured the Cross . . .' **Hebrews 12:2**.

**Hebrews** is all about the ascended Christ. Jesus' third anointing happened after the Cross, it was an anointing of joy, part of His 'adoption' as an heir, as the victorious Son.

## The Son and Heir

**Psalm 2** started with kings and rulers contending with the Messiah. It ends advising kings and judges to be wise . . .

Worship *YHWH* with reverence . . . Kiss / give homage to the Son . . . Blessed are all who take refuge in him. **Psalm 2:11–12**

Honour God, honour the Son, be blessed! Jesus states the same in John's Gospel:

That all may honour the Son, even as they honour the Father . . . Truly, truly, I say to you, whoever hears My word and believes . . . has eternal life. **John 5:23**

Salvation has always been by faith in Jesus even before people knew Him by that name.

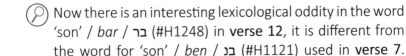

Now there is an interesting lexicological oddity in the word 'son' / *bar* / בר (#H1248) in **verse 12**, it is different from the word for 'son' / *ben* / בן (#H1121) used in **verse 7**.

In David's day, *bar* was a foreign word, though it would have been recognised by Hebrew readers.

My favourite approach to solving this puzzle is to recognise that foreign words often enter a language as titles before they become part of the vernacular. In English we use foreign titles such as *attaché* or *aide de camp* and this seems to be how *bar* is used here and in the book of **Daniel** (see 'Son of God', **Daniel 3:25**; 'Son of Man', **Daniel 7:13**). So as a title, *Bar* is a 'Son' for the whole world, not just ethnic Israelites.

**Psalm 2** started with the formal 'adoption' of God's Son as heir, and finished with a Son for everyone seated in the heavenly senate judging the whole world. It is a wonderfully full introduction to the *Messianic Psalms*.

## Psalm 18 – The Horn of Salvation

The second **Psalm** to mention the Messiah is a tidied-up version of the song sung by David in **2 Samuel 22**. It summed up David's long period of conflicts with Saul, the nations around him, his own people and even his own son.

The word Messiah appears in its last verse. In the same sentence we find the name 'Jesus' / ישוע hidden in the word 'deliverance' which is in the feminine plural form, ישועות. Jesus' name is extended with a wav-ו and then a tav-ת. In *Volume 1: Jesus in the Old Testament* we saw how and why these letters were understood and originally depicted as a peg / nail Y, and by crossed sticks +, respectively. We can think of 'deliverance' as Jesus-fixed-to-a-cross!

> Make great the great deliverance [Jesus-fixed-to-a-cross] of His King and kindness to His *Anointed-Messiah*, to David and to His descendant forever. **Psalm 18:50**

The **Psalm** brings David's years of conflict to an end with the Messiah and a word that shows Jesus-fixed-to-a-cross!

But Jesus would have meditated on this **Psalm** as He grew, not for its ending but for the way it begins – with the title 'the Horn of my Salvation' (see **verse 2**). This unique title was given to Jesus while He was still in the womb, **Luke 1:69**.

So Jesus grew up with the **Psalm**, you can see its influence in the Sermon on the Mount!

- 'With the merciful, you show yourself merciful', **Psalm 18:25a**, or as Jesus puts it, 'Blessed are the merciful, for they shall receive mercy', **Matthew 5:7**.

- 'With the pure, you show yourself pure', **Psalm18:26a**, and Jesus says, 'Blessed are the pure in heart, for they shall see God', **Matthew 5:8**.

But let's start at the beginning with that pre-birth prophecy.

> [*YHWH*] has raised up a **Horn of Salvation** for us in the house of David his servant . . . Salvation from our enemies from the hand of all who hate us. Luke 1:69–71

Zecharias is speaking at the birth of John the Baptist, but the 'Horn of Salvation' is the Messiah. Zecharias' family were priests, descendants of Aaron, not David. But over the previous three months Mary has been visiting Zecharias' wife Elizabeth. Mary was part of David's line, and she was pregnant with Jesus (salvation).

So, it is interesting that Zecharias continues with: 'Salvation from our enemies from the hand of all who hate us'. It is a quote from **Psalm 106:10**, which follows a request for a visit, 'Remember me O Lord . . . visit me with your salvation [Jesus] . . . ', **Psalm106:4**.

Zecharias had just lived the answer to this request, because 'salvation' is *yshua* / ישוע, or 'Jesus', Zechariah's recent houseguest. (Note: the title 'Horn of Salvation' contains only the shorter version ישע rather than ישוע, see **Psalm 20**).

Zecharias was a priest, well versed in Scripture, so his prophecy, the title, and the **Psalms** he referenced became a part of Jesus' family history. **Psalm 18** contains words that spoke about Jesus' Crucifixion.

> The cords of death encompassed me, floods of ungodliness [*Belial*] troubled me. The cords

of Sheol surrounded me; the snares of death confronted me. In my distress I called upon the Lord, and cried to my God for help. **Psalm18:4–6a**

Now *Belial* translated here as 'ungodliness' became personified as a demonic force in Jewish thinking. One of the Dead Sea Scrolls tells us: '[*Belial's*] counsel is to bring about wickedness and guilt'.

On the Cross, Jesus is overwhelmed by the demonic force of the world's ungodliness, and '. . . cried out with a loud voice . . . "My God, my God" . . . ', **Mark 15:34**.

The **Psalm** continues with some good news: 'He heard my voice out of His Temple and my cry for help . . . came into His ears. Then the earth shook and quaked', **Psalm18:6b–7a.**

 So, we read in **Matthew**: 'Then Jesus cried out again with a loud voice . . . then the Temple curtain was torn in two, from top to bottom. The earth shook and the rocks were split apart,' **Matthew 27:50–51**.

When David wrote these words, the Temple was still a dream. David connects to a future hope in worship. In his prophetic ecstasy David continues: 'He bowed the heavens and came down with thick darkness . . . thick clouds of the sky', **Psalm18:9–11**.

And Matthew tells us: 'Now from noon until three, darkness came over all the land', **Matthew 27:45**.

In the **Psalm** *YHWH* hears the Messiah's cry: 'He sent from on high, He took me; He drew me out of many waters. He delivered me from my strong enemy', **Psalm18:16–17a**.

In the ancient world 'waters' were symbolic of things beyond human control; of chaos, death and even the demonic of *Belial* as the **Psalm** has already put it!

Jesus would have to go into the waters of death before He would be drawn out of them, 'He brought me into a broad place, He drew me out because He was pleased with me', **Psalm 18:19**.

Jesus had heard His Father's pleasure in Him as He was drawn out of the Jordan in Baptism, it kept this **Psalm** relevant as He was engulfed in the ungodly chaos of the Crucifixion.

It is the nature of ecstatic prophecy to blend the prophet's experience with the Passion of Jesus. And there is a lot more in **Psalm 18** that feels like it was written for or about Jesus – you may want to re-read it all before we continue. You'll notice it has a connection with the next *Messianic Psalm* too!

 This is a good point to transfer some notes into your Bible

# Psalm 20 – Praying for Holy Help

The third *Messianic Psalm* is short and focused. It starts with an idea from **Psalm 18**, but with a changed perspective.

> May the name of the God of Jacob protect you, may He send you help from the Holy Place and support from Zion . . . He [*YHWH*] will answer Him [the Messiah] from His Holy Heaven.
> **Psalm 20:1b–2,6b**

In **Psalm 18** the Messiah called out to God who answered from the Temple and from Heaven. In **Psalm 20** God's people pray for help and support for the Messiah from the Holy Place and from Heaven.

It was a prayer to be sung and said by everybody and it made them prayer participants in the Messiah's victory, while expressing faith in Jesus.

> We will sing for joy in your victory [Jesus / ישועת] and in the name of our God, we will set up our banners. **Psalm 20:5a**

The Hebrew word for 'victory' is Jesus' name with a tav-ת, a cross-✝, at the end of it. The singer declares by faith that they will rally around Jesus-cross. Then they add their prayers to those of the Messiah, 'May *YHWH* fulfil all your petitions', **Psalm 20:5c**.

John's Gospel records Jesus' prayers as He accepts the challenge of the Cross in Gethsemane:

> He [Jesus] looked up to Heaven and said: 'Father, the time has come. Glorify your Son, so that your Son may glorify you . . . I ask on their behalf . . .' **John 17:1a, 9a**

Jesus' petition was for us, and it included:

> . . . keep them in your name which you have given Me . . . that they may have My joy made full in themselves . . . **John 17:11b, 13b**

Joy in the Jesus-cross and in God's name is part of the worshippers' song. They continue by singing:

> Now I know that *YHWH* saves His **Anointed-Messiah**, He will answer from His Holy Heaven in the masterful-act of salvation [Jesus] His right hand. **Psalm 20:6b–c**

This 'salvation' is the informal version of Jesus' name, *Ysha /* ישע, which the Syrian Peshitta preserves as Jesus' name for us (see *Volume 1: Jesus in the Old Testament*).

Jesus' masterful-act is the Cross, it is the saving of God by God but for us! Or as Jesus prays in Gethsemane, 'for their sakes I sanctify Myself, so that they can be sanctified', **John 17:19**.

In **Psalm 20**, those that sing 'I know that *YHWH* saves His **Anointed-Messiah**' express hope for themselves in the last line:

> May the King [the-Messiah] answer us in the day we call. **Psalm 20:9b**

## Psalm 28 – A Refuge of Jesus

The theme of the Messiah's prayers for Himself and for His people continues in the fourth *Messianic Psalm*. **Psalm 28** starts with the distress and prayers of the Messiah but finishes with blessings and promise for the people.

> To you, O *YHWH*, I cry out! My rock, do not ignore me! Unless you respond to me, I will join those who are descending into the grave. **Psalm 28:1**

With hindsight we can see Crucifixion imagery in the next verse:

> Hear the voice of my pleas for mercy, when I cry to you for help, when I lift up my hands toward your most holy sanctuary. **Psalm 28:2**

Jesus was crucified just outside Jerusalem within sight of the Temple. He was nailed to the Cross in a way that inadvertently mimicked the outspread, and uplifted hands of supplication prayer.

We have seen in the previous two **Messianic Psalms** that this prayer is answered, and as we read on we find:

> Blessed be *YHWH*, He has heard the voice of my petitions. **Psalm 28:6**

But the focus now shifts to the benefits to God's people, not just the Messiah:

> *YHWH* is *their* strength and He is a strong place of salvation [Jesus-fixed-to-a-cross], His Anointed-Messiah. **Psalm 28:6–8**

'Salvation' is in its plural form ישועות which, we saw in **Psalm 18**, is Jesus' name extended with a wav-ו and a tav-ת, a nail and a cross. The strong place of salvation is the Messiah's Cross!

The **Psalm** ends:

> Save your people and bless your inheritance and be their shepherd and carry them for ever. **Psalm 28:9**

## Psalm 84 – God Appears with the Messiah

The fifth *Messianic Psalm* is one of eleven **Psalms** attributed to the sons of Korah.

Like all the Korahite Psalms it is full of beautiful imagery. It is a grateful eulogy on the blessings of 'the one who trusts in you [*YHWH*]', **Psalm 84:12**. It would be unremarkable except for a single line that is lost in some modern translations of the Bible.

The New Revised Standard Version follows the older Hebrew manuscripts and the Septuagint (the Ancient Greek Version of the Bible). It reads:

> They go from strength to strength; *the God of gods will be seen in Zion*. **Psalm 84:7**

As the righteous hunger for the dwelling place of God, the **Psalm** anticipates a time when the 'highway' in people's hearts (**Psalm 84:5**) makes a way for *YHWH* Himself to appear.

**Verses 5 to 7** reflect the verses from **Isaiah 40** that became John the Baptist's message: 'Make ready the way of the Lord', **Matthew 3:3c**.

| Psalm 84 | Isaiah 40 |
|---|---|
| How blessed is the man . . . in whose heart are the highways to Zion. **(v5)** | . . . clear the way for *YHWH*, make smooth in the desert a highway for our God. **(v3)** |
| . . . they make the valley of weeping a spring, the early rain covers it with blessing. **(v6)** | Let every valley be lifted up . . . the rugged terrain a broad valley. **(v4)** |

| . . . the God of gods will be seen in Zion. **(v7)** | . . . so that the Glory of *YHWH* will be revealed, and all flesh will see it together. **(v5)** |
|---|---|

The parallel imagery with **Isaiah 40** is striking, so it is sad that so many translations break the symmetry by translating **verse 7** as something like: 'Every one of them appears before God'. They do so because of a small change to the Hebrew text made over a thousand years after it was originally written.

Between the seventh and ninth centuries AD, a Jewish sect, the Masoretes, 'tidied up' the Hebrew text of the Bible, adding vowel pointers for vocalisation and deciding how words should be grouped or divided.

In the older texts of **Psalm 84:7** we find two words *El Elohim* / אל אלהים meaning 'God of gods'. The Masoretic text made this a single compound word, *El:Elohim* / אל:אלהים meaning *'to* God'. Now the 'tidied up' Hebrew doesn't read as smoothly as the original, so translators infer extra words such as 'each one' or 'every one of them' into the verse to help it make sense.

This text change hadn't happened in Jesus' day. Everybody understood this verse to mean that, one day, God would appear, and the Messiah would be present as well, because the **Psalm** goes on:

> See our shield *Elohim*, and look on the presence of your Anointed-Messiah. **Psalm 84:9**

The Messiah is 'our shield', but **verse 11** tells us that '*YHWH Elohim* is a sun and shield . . . ' To see God is to see the Messiah and vice-versa.

**Psalm 84** is a prophecy of THE future theophany!

 ## Psalm 89 – The Messiah's Heels are Pierced

 **Psalm 89** is by Ethan the Ezrahite, one of David's advisers (**1 Kings 4:31**). A gifted musician (**1 Chronicles 15:19**), he helped to install the Ark in the Tabernacle of David, a place the New Testament treats as a prophetic type of Jesus (see *Volume 7: Jesus in the United Nation* and *Volume 12: Jesus in the Minor Prophets*).

 In the **Psalm** *YHWH* addresses 'My Chosen', 'David' whose 'seed' He will establish forever on a throne for all generations, **Psalm 89:3–4**. It contains several verses that illuminate Jesus' story. For instance:

 > You rule the raging of the sea. When its waves rise up you calm them. **Psalm 89:9**

This is one of several verses in the **Psalms** to refer to *YHWH* stilling the waves of a storm (see **Psalm 65:5–7**, **89:9**, **107:29**), a truth modelled by Jesus in the late summer / early autumn of 31 AD illustrating His Divinity (**Matthew 8:26**, **Mark 4:39**, **Luke 8:24**). Then we read:

He will call to me, 'You are my Father, my God, and the rock of my salvation [Jesus-with-a-cross/ישועת]' I will make him firstborn-most-high to the Kings of the earth. **Psalm 89:26–27**

David's promised descendant will be *YHWH*'s firstborn and the highest authority on earth.

The final movement of **Psalm 89** is a lament on how *YHWH*'s loved and chosen Messiah is rejected, spurned and cut off from Him. It starts:

But You [*YHWH*] have cast off and rejected. You have been estranged from your *Anointed-Messiah*. **Psalm 89:38**

You can read everything that follows into the Cross, but it is the last mention of the Messiah that gives **Psalm 89** its impact. The Messiah asks prophetically:

What man can live and not see death? Can he deliver his soul from the power of the grave? **Psalm 89:48**

He responds to the question by looking for God's kindness and requesting:

My Lord, remember the cutting taunts of your servants, I carry within me all the many people. In this way *YHWH*, your enemies have pierced, in this way they have pierced the heels of your Anointed-Messiah. **Psalm 89:50–51**

You are not likely to have seen this verse translated this way before!

But lexicological analysis shows that the words for 'cutting taunts', *cherpah* / חרפה (#H2781) and for 'pierced', *charaph* / חרף (#H2778) are part of a word group for things that are all connected by 'cutting' or 'piercing'.

English translations make the meanings abstract, translating the former as 'rebukes' or 'scorns', and the latter as 'reproached' or 'upbraided'. But Hebrew is a concrete language, so *The Ancient Hebrew Lexicon of the Bible* suggests the use of 'piercing' for *charaph* / חרף (see AHLB #2208).

So, the Messiah carries within Himself 'all the many people', and those who are called *YHWH*'s servants are actually 'piercing' the Messiah, even piercing His 'heels' ('footsteps' in some translations).

The Romans often crucified by nailing through the heel rather than the flat of the foot. Jesus' heels were pierced as He carried the sin of the many in Himself on the Cross.

There is a final verse, but is not part of the **Psalm** proper. It is the section break between books three and four of the **Psalms** (see also **Psalm 41:13, 72:19–20, 89:52, 106:48**).

So the last proper line of Ethan's song ecstatically captures the Crucifixion: they have pierced the heels of your Anointed-Messiah!

# Psalm 105 – The Messiah is Multiplied

Technically, **Psalm 105** doesn't refer to 'the Messiah', it refers to 'Messiahs': 'Do not touch my Messiahs and do my prophets no harm', **Psalm105:15**.

Whether **Psalm 105** should be considered a *Messianic Psalm* or not is a bit ambiguous. With it there are eight *Messianic Psalms*, without it there are just seven. We saw in *Volume 2: Jesus in the Beginning* how often a list of seven things promised an eighth related but new thing, and then we saw in *Volume 7: Jesus in the United Nation* how David himself was both the seventh and eighth son of Jessie.

Perhaps the ambiguity works to show us more!

The Church quoted the first *Messianic Psalm* as it relived Jesus' persecution experience (**Acts 4:24–27**, quoting **Psalm 2:1–2**). Then they prayed:

> 'Lord take note of their threats' . . . and when they had prayed, the place . . . was shaken and they were all filled with the Holy Spirit and they spoke the word of God with boldness. **Acts 4:29–31**

The New Testament Church knew the truth of 'Christ in us', it included His suffering as well as the hope of glory, **Romans 8:18** and **Colossians 1:27**. As they reproduced Jesus' experience it brought them into His anointing too.

In **Psalm 105**, *YHWH*'s anointing has been multiplied to protect His prophets, those that speak boldly for Him!

There is a bit more on how anointing is multiplied in the last *Messianic Psalm* too.

 Psalm 132 – A Lamp for the Messiah

 **Psalm 132**, the seventh **Psalm** to mention the Messiah or the eighth *Messianic Psalm*, is a prayer for blessing on *YHWH*'s dwelling place. It draws on the story of David taking the Ark of the Covenant up to Zion to find it a suitable home. The **Psalm** reminds God to remember David 'the Messiah' (**verse 10**) and His promise to set a physical descendant on David's throne.

Towards the end of the **Psalm** it uses the title 'Messiah' for a second time, declaring:

> This is my resting place forever, here I will dwell
> . . . her priests I will clothe with salvation and her
> saints will sing aloud for joy. There I will cause the
> horn of David to bud, I have prepared a lamp for
> my *Anointed-Messiah*. **Psalm 132:14, 16–17**

Jesus was called 'the Horn of Salvation . . . in the house of David' by Zecharias when he prophesied over his son John the Baptist, **Luke 1:69**. A horn was a symbol of power or leadership, but horns were also used to carry and administer anointing oil (see **1 Samuel 16:1,13**; **1 Kings 1:39**; **Psalm 92:10**). Leadership and authority came from that anointing, and 'the Horn of David' refers to the commission that was on him.

Now, in the **Psalm** we read that the horn will 'bud'. In nature horns don't bud, trees and plants do. Things bud as they are about to reproduce and multiply. So, the budding of 'the horn of David' means that the anointing of David is about to multiply and bear fruit.

 **Psalm 132** is giving us details about how 'the Messiah' becomes the 'Messiahs' of **Psalm 105**: 'her [the future Temple] priests I will clothe with salvation [Jesus]', **Psalm 132:16**. 'Salvation' is the shortened version of Jesus' name (ישע rather than ישוע, see **Psalms 18 and 20**), but it is His name. So, in **Psalm 132**:

- God has a permanent dwelling place, **v14**
- Where the ministers are clothed in 'Jesus', **v16**
- Anointing will multiply, **v17a**
- And this place will be a lamp for his Messiah, **v17b**

In the **New Testament**:

- We are 'being built together into a dwelling place of God', **Ephesians 2:22**
- Paul tells us to 'put on the Lord Jesus Christ', **Romans 13:4**
- On the day of Pentecost 3000 received the Holy Spirit, **Acts 2:38, 41**
- Jesus Himself calls us 'the light of the world', **Matthew 5:14**

Perhaps in these last two *Messianic Psalms* we see the mystery of Christ in us, **Colossians 1:27**, the multiplication of the image of Jesus in His people, His Church.

# The Messianic Psalms in Conclusion

As Jesus grew in His understanding of Himself the *Messianic Psalms* would have spoken to Him with increasing clarity. He would have had to face the implications of His own suffering found in them, as well as the hints of a future hope, legacy and multiplication. They present Jesus clearly and cryptically. They are all typological, they are about the 'Anointed'. Several are written by Jesus' forebear David. They contain prophecy, things that Jesus taught, hints at His Divinity and even a theophany.

They encompass everything we find in the whole of the **Psalms**, but they are not everything that the **Psalms** have to say about Jesus!

This is a good point to transfer some notes into your Bible

# Part 2

## Prophecy in the Psalms

Biblical prophecy is by nature more forthtelling than foretelling. God-breathed it creates and corrals history towards and through provident moments without dictating every detail of how to travel. *Predictive Psalms* set the signposts that tell us we are getting close to the climax of the current movement.

We will consider two **Psalms** in detail that make significant predictions, one has been 'fulfilled', the other is still future.

## Psalm 41 – Close-knit Friends

In Gethsemane Jesus prays:

> And none of them is lost except that son of lostness,
> so that Scripture would be fulfilled. **John 17:12b**

**Psalm 41** doesn't predict the irreversible lostness of Judas. There is no prophecy of that anywhere, only the betrayal of a friend, as Jesus points out . . .

> . . . I know those I have chosen, and that the
> Scripture may be fulfilled, 'He who eats bread with
> me has lifted his heel against me.' **John 13:18**

Jesus' words and subsequent actions are an appeal to Judas, because 'the Son of Man came to save that which was lost', **Matthew 18:11**. Jesus offers him forgiveness, it's Judas' pride that dooms him.

**Psalm 41** describes a time when David is unwell, and his enemies are making the most of his illness. As David cries out to *YHWH*, his words become a prophecy with more in it than just a betrayal. But it is the betrayal that makes it stand out.

Jesus washes the disciples' feet because they've been discussing their relative greatness, **Luke 22:24**. But as they each lift their feet to Jesus, He sees **Psalm 41** in progress and is troubled before quoting and acting out the prophecy by sharing bread with Judas, **John 13:21–26**.

As events unfold, there is plenty in the **Psalm** that Jesus would have drawn strength from: '*YHWH* will preserve him' **v2**, 'raise me up' **v10**, 'you uphold me . . . and set me in your presence forever', **v12**.

There are also lines describing Judas and the plan he made:

> Those that hate me are whispering together against me, they weave evil for me. Saying 'An evil (Belial) word is poured into him, when he lies down he shall not rise up again'. Even my close friend who I trusted and who ate my bread has lifted his heel against me. **Psalm 41:7–9**

The words translated 'close friend', are actually 'man of peace'. Later that same evening Judas would greet Jesus with a sign of peace, a kiss.

And an 'evil word' (sometimes translated 'evil disease') is literally a 'word of Belial'. We met Belial in **Psalm 18** (pages 19–21), a demonic force 'to bring about wickedness and guilt'. So a 'word of Belial' would be a curse that imputed wickedness and guilt, even in someone without sin.

Or as **Galatians** puts it:

> Christ redeemed us from the curse of the law, having become a curse for us. **Galatians 3:13a**

And there is a remarkable hidden reference to the Last Supper in these verses too.

Starting at 'they weave' / *ichashab* / יחשבו (#H2803) we find Jesus' name ישוע interwoven every other letter with two other Hebrew words. The first, *chaber* / חבר means 'companion' (#H2269) or 'knitted together' (#H2270). But if we add the next letter in the sentence the word becomes *chabrah* / חברח which means 'the company that ate Passover together'. See below.

Those that hate me are whispering together
against me, they weave evil for me. **Psalm 41:7**

← ——————————Read Hebrew Right to Left——————————

| לי | רעה | יחשבו | עלי | שנאי | כל | יתלחשו | עלי | יחר |
|---|---|---|---|---|---|---|---|---|
| for-me | evil | they-are-twisting | on-me | ones-hating-me | all-of | they-are-whispering | on-me | together |

Jesus is interwoven with His Passover-company and is knitted together with a close friend who is twisting evil against Him!

Jesus' name is hidden again in the next two verses. This time spread out every fourteenth letter starting with the first yod-י in the penultimate word of **verse 8** 'he-shall'/ יוסיף (#H3254). Fourteen is the gematric value of the name 'David', who wrote this **Psalm**. I will leave you to trace this for yourself.

## Psalm 45 - The Joy of the Bridegroom

**Psalm 45** doesn't refer directly to '*The* Messiah', but it is addressed to someone who has been anointed, **Psalm 45:7b**.

It was written to celebrate a king's wedding, one who is blessed forever, **Psalm 45:2**. It is a song for 'the bridegroom', an epithet Jesus gives to Himself, **Mark 2:19–20**.

The title has a prophetic pedigree. Three times, Jeremiah tells us that 'the bridegroom' and the 'sound of his joy and gladness' will be taken away, **Jeremiah 7:34**, **16:9**, **25:10**, before his happy return in the days when David's heir sits forever on David's throne, **Jeremiah 33:11,15,17**.

**Psalm 45** can be read as predictive of Jesus' second coming, the marriage of the Lamb and His Bride. Of the bridegroom we read, 'Grace is poured through your lips . . .' , **Psalm 45:2a**. With Jesus we read '. . . all . . . were wondering at the gracious words which were proceeding from His mouth', **Luke 4:22**.

The book of **Hebrews** makes the connection between **Psalm 45** and Jesus much more explicit. In fact, it presents the whole Trinity as present in this **Psalm** - I've added Father, Son and Spirit to make it obvious.

> . . . of the Son he says: 'Your throne O God [the-Son] is forever and ever . . . so God [the-Father] Your [the-Son's] God [the-Father] has anointed you [the-Son] with the Oil of Joy [the-Spirit] above your [the-Son's] companions.
> **Hebrews 1:8–9**, quoting **Psalm 45:6–8**

As **Hebrews** develops it tells us that, '. . . Jesus . . . for the joy set before him, endured the Cross', **Hebrews 12:2**.

The fullness of the anointing of joy belongs to a period beyond Jesus' death and resurrection mirroring the loss and return of the bridegroom's joy in **Jeremiah**. While **Psalm 45** belongs to the age of Jesus' return, we find a hint of His death in the **Psalm** too.

> All your garments are fragrant with myrrh, aloes, and cassia, **Psalm 45:8**

As Jesus' body is removed from the Cross, Nicodemus steps forward to provide myrrh and aloes to dress the body, **John 19:39**, and the women agree to buy additional spices once the markets re-open after the Sabbath, **Mark 16:1**.

Nicodemus has provided 100 pounds in weight of myrrh and aloes, worth more than three times a normal salary. So the women would not have bought more myrrh and aloes, but they would almost certainly have bought cassia.

**In Psalm 45, the bridegroom's robes are soaked in Jesus' burial spices!**

And there is something else to note about cassia. First, in the Hebrew text, there is no 'and' to join it to 'myrrh and aloes', it is as though 'cassia' is a separate idea; Second, this is not the regular word for cassia, קדה / *kde* (#H6916), it is the word *ktziah* / קציעה (#H7102/3).

*Ktziah* only appears one other time in the Old Testament, it is a name, 'Kezia', a daughter restored to Job after his troubles, **Job 42:14**.

I have daughter called Kezia, so I know the word's etymology.

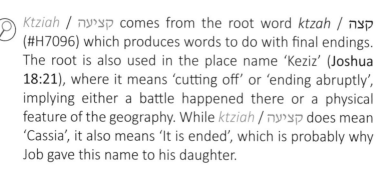

*Ktziah* / קציעה comes from the root word *ktzah* / קצה (#H7096) which produces words to do with final endings. The root is also used in the place name 'Keziz' (**Joshua 18:21**), where it means 'cutting off' or 'ending abruptly', implying either a battle happened there or a physical feature of the geography. While *ktziah* / קציעה does mean 'Cassia', it also means 'It is ended', which is probably why Job gave this name to his daughter.

Translating *ktziah* / קציעה this way in **Psalm 45** (and reflecting the missing 'and') gives:

> All your garments are fragrant with myrrh and aloes, it is ended! **Psalm 45:8**

From the Cross, Jesus says, 'It is finished', then His body is clothed in myrrh and aloes, **John 19:30,39–40**.

This is a good point to transfer some notes into your Bible

# Ecstatic Prophecy

Ecstatic prophecy happens when the emotion and events of Jesus' Passion break into the psalmist's reverie. **Psalm 22** is by David, but there is nothing in David's experience that resembles it. However, it does describe the Crucifixion moment by moment.

## Psalm 22 – A Sign of Salvation

**Psalm 22** is 230 Hebrew words long and the 115th word is 'they-enclose-me' / *eqiphuni* / הקיפוני. Enclosing this midpoint we find the phrase 'They pierced my hands and my feet' on one side, and on the other a hidden message. Ending in the 114th word, 'evildoers', every twenty-sixth Hebrew letter spells out the phrase:

> *awth k-yshua* / אות כישוע, which means: 'A Sign like Jesus'

Twenty-six is the gematric value of the name *YHWH* / יהוה (Y=10, H=5, W=6, H=5). It is as though God has deliberately left His fingerprint in the very middle of **Psalm 22** for us to find.

The table below highlights the words that encode each letter of that hidden message. You may want to highlight them in your Bible.

*'A Sign like Jesus' in Psalm 22*

| Verse | Word/phrase | Hebrew word | Every 26th Letter |
|-------|-------------|-------------|-------------------|
| 11 | 'Be not' | אל | א – A |
| 11 | 'none to help' | עוזר | ו – W |
| 12 | 'encircled' | כתרוני | ת – Th |
| 14 | 'like water' | כמים | כ – K |
| 14 | 'are' | היה | י – Y |
| 15 | 'potsherd' | כחרש | ש – Sh |
| 15 | 'death' | מות | ו – U |
| 16 | 'evil doers' | מרעים | ע – A |

The first word in this hidden phrase, *Awth* / אות (#H226), is always used for God's saving grace. We saw in *Volume 2: Jesus in the Beginning* how it was originally written in Hebrew's ancient pictographic script as a bull (a big sacrifice), a nail/peg and a cross:

$$+YV$$

*Awth* is the mark that makes something genuine, here it acts as God's signature hidden in the **Psalm**.

Jesus spoke just seven times from the Cross, each sentence required Him to lift Himself to exhale. The fourth time with great effort Jesus shouted the opening phrase of **Psalm 22**, because it was a 'sign like Him' and it said what Jesus could not!

 As Jesus' hearers heard 'My God, my God, why have you forsaken me?' (**v1a**) they would have supplied the **Psalm's** next line from memory: 'Why are you so far from my Jesus (salvation)?' (**v1b**). David asks the question for many in the crowd. With regards to the Cross, David has shifted his perspective from feeling it to seeing it, that is the nature of Ecstatic prophecy.

David's question is not an accusation; it is immediately followed by an expression of faith in God's holiness and faithfulness, **Psalm 22:3–5**.

David again feels the ignominy of the Cross, and says 'But I am a worm, and not a man', **Psalm 22:6**. By the Spirit he uses a word with a double meaning. The word for 'worm', *towla* / תולע (#H8348), is more often translated 'scarlet' or 'crimson' than it is 'worm'. It is often used with another Hebrew word with the same set of meanings, *shaniy* / שני (#H8144):

> . . . though your sins be as scarlet (*shaniy* / שני),
> they shall be as white as snow; though they be
> red like crimson (*towla* / תולע), they shall be as
> wool. Isaiah 1:18

Both words can be a 'red colour', a 'red dye' or the 'red grub' that makes the red dye.

This worm is the pupa stage of the *Coccus ilicus* (or *Kermes ilicus*), an insect that mirrors the Gospel in its life-cycle. The female never develops into a crawling insect, instead the pupa fuses itself to the branch of a tree and becomes bloated with a red antiseptic fluid (making it less palatable to predators). Eggs are laid and hatch under this swollen covering. They are washed in the antiseptic 'blood' and their first meal is part of the mother's own body. As Isaiah says of the Suffering Servant:

> His shape was disfigured more than anyone's . . .
> so he shall sprinkle many peoples. Isaiah 52:14

 **Psalm 22** continues by saying that this bloated-blood-red-worm-fused-to-a-tree is a 'reproach' at whom people 'wag their heads'. He is mocked with the words, 'Commit

yourself to *YHWH*! Let *YHWH* rescue him! . . . because He delights in him,' **Psalm 22:7–8**.

We find these words paralleled in the Gospels:

> Those passing by were abusing Him, wagging their heads and saying '. . . let Him come down from the Cross now, and we will believe in Him. He trusts in God. Let God deliver Him now, if He wants Him.' **Matthew 27:39–43**

Then **Psalm 22** shifts its focus to 'my mother's womb' and 'my mother's breasts . . .' (**v9–10**). On the Cross we read how Jesus broke from His own pain to address that of His mother: '. . . when Jesus saw His mother . . . standing there . . . He said . . .', **John 19:26**.

**Verses 11 to 16** contain the hidden phrase 'A Sign like Jesus', but there are other features to note in these verses as well.

First, there is the surrounding presence of 'bulls' (**v12**), 'lions' (**v13**) and 'dogs' (**v16**). The same three animals appear again in **verses 20–21** and collectively they are the 'band of evildoers' that pierce the victim's hands and feet (**v16**). All three images can simply represent the adversarial powers and authorities that conspired and spectated the Crucifixion. But there is a more nuanced symbolism in them too. In the ancient world (and reflected in Scripture) we find that:

- Bulls represent demonic powers. From Hathor and the Apis Bull in Ancient Egypt, right up to manifestations of Zeus in the Greek myths of Jesus' day, a bull was the most enduring image for a pagan god. It was even the image the Israelites adopted as an idol of *YHWH*. Both the Old Testament and the New are explicit in identifying these gods as demons, **Deuteronomy 32:17** and **1 Corinthians 10:20**. The devil was present in the events of Jesus' death, **John 13:2**.

On the Cross, Jesus was surrounded by demonic powers.

– Lions in the ancient world were symbols of military leaders and powers. There is archaeological evidence that Saul was nicknamed the Lion, and David refers to him as 'a lion that wants to tear its prey to bits', **Psalm 17:12**. **Proverbs** refers to rulers and kings as lions (**Proverbs 19:12, 20:2, 28:15**) and **Isaiah 5:29** prophesies about Assyria's military power as a lion.

On the Cross, Jesus was surrounded by the military might of Rome.

– Dogs came to be symbolic of the Gentiles. We find this nomenclature in Jesus' conversation with the Syrophoenician woman, **Mark 7:27**. By the time we reach **Revelation** the term refers more specifically to *those that have rejected the Good News*, **Revelation 22:15**.

On the Cross, Jesus was surrounded by Gentiles and those that had rejected the Good News.

Next, **verse 14** starts with the statement, 'I am poured out like water', **Psalm 22:14a**. This 'poured out' is different from the word we looked at in **Psalm 2** where it was a careful and constructive pouring into or onto. Here the word is *shaphak* / שפך (#H8210) which describes the state of something that has been spilt, splashed or tipped on the ground.

 *Shaphak* / שפך is what happened to the blood given to God from a sin or burnt offering, **Leviticus 4:7** and **Deuteronomy 12:27**. And the blood of every firstborn animal of a flock was 'poured out', before its body fed the household, both the ceremonially clean and unclean alike, **Deuteronomy 15:19–23**.

It is an appropriate word for Jesus' loss of blood at his Crucifixion. The Roman 'flagellum' or 'flagrum' whips used for scourging had three or more thongs weighted with lead and stone. They were designed to break open the flesh by blunt force rather than by slicing; to create a slow but constant bleed from deep wounds rather than a gushing loss of blood which would kill the victim before their formal execution.

On the Cross, Jesus bled slowly but constantly. The four 'horns' of His altar were marked by the wounds on His head, hands and feet, while blood from His back was poured out at its base.

Jesus' death re-enacted the sin offering offered by Moses to consecrate a new priesthood!

> He [Moses] brought the bull of the sin offering
> . . . slaughtered it and took the blood . . . and put
> it on the horns of the altar . . . then he poured
> out (*shaphak* / שפך) the rest of the blood at
> the base of the altar, making atonement for it.
> **Leviticus 8:14–15**

You see, the root of the Hebrew word 'horns' used of the altar, simply means 'things-that-stick-out'. It can mean a 'ray' or 'wing', **Malachi 4:2**, even 'a hill', **Isaiah 5:1**. It could even be the spars that stick-out-from a cross!

It was the Persians who first invented crucifixion, but the Romans perfected it to maximise and prolong its pain. They bent their victim's legs and nailed their feet in a position that required constant muscle exertion to support the body on a small ledge at the base of the spine. Balancing took effort and regular adjustment and without support it was hard to breathe.

When you slipped your weight jarred your chest and arms. Limbs were wrenched at odd angles pulling elbows and wrists out of joint. In a short period this process could add 20 cm to the length of the victim's arms. **Psalm 22:14** continues: 'All my bones are out of joint'.

Each dislocation was grotesquely exaggerated as Jesus struggled for balance and breath. The spectacle is described a few verses later, 'I can count all my bones, they look, they stare at me!', **Psalm 22:17**.

But before that we read, 'My heart is like wax; it is melted within me', **Psalm 22:14c.**

Jesus died of a heart attack. 'Blood and water' (**John 19:34**) are evidence of both pulmonary oedema (fluid in the lungs) and/or pericardial effusion (fluid from the sac that surrounds the heart), both are signs of a heart attack. Severe thirst can precede a heart attack. Jesus says, 'I am thirsty', **John 19:28** and **Psalm 22:15** states: 'My strength is dried up like a potsherd, my tongue sticks to my mouth.'

As Jesus' blood slowly drained from Him, His blood pressure would have dropped dramatically and His body would have instinctively started drawing water from less critical systems to replace essential blood flow. The result is extreme and painful dehydration, while the heart beats faster and faster to compensate for the low blood pressure. As the heart approaches two beats a second, trauma in the pericardium builds up plasma and blood. This surrounding fluid pressurises from the outside the already frenetic heart until it ruptures. Jesus' heart melted within Him.

> They pierced my hands and my feet. **Psalm 22:16b**

This phrase, in the very middle of the **Psalm**, would mark it as prophetic of Jesus even if He hadn't quoted it from the Cross. Perhaps unsurprisingly the verse is not without controversy and occasionally you will find a translation that reads: 'like a lion, my hands and feet'. The New Revised

Standard Version has 'my hands and feet have shrivelled' with a note that the Hebrew is not clear. So, what is going on and can we be confident that the traditional translation is correct?

The confusion arises because the Hebrew for 'they pierced', *carah* / כרו (#H3738) is almost identical to 'like a lion' / כארי (prefixed version of #H738). You can get 'like a lion' from 'they pierced' by adding one letter and shortening the stem on the wav-ו to make it a yod-י.

Now the only ancient fragment and every ancient commentary we have on **Psalm 22** reads 'they pierced my hands and feet' or something similar, as does the Ancient Greek Septuagint. But most (though not all) Hebrew Masoretic texts read 'like a lion, my hands and feet' even though this is bad grammar, as the phrase lacks a verb.

The Masoretic texts date from the tenth century, a thousand years after Jesus, and a time when the Christian Church often persecuted the Jewish community. It seems that the change crept into the Hebrew text through a combination of scribal error and a desire in the Jewish community to distance their Bible from that of the dominant Christian Church.

Strangely, while 'like a lion, my hands and feet' is probably a corruption of the original Hebrew text, it still fits crucifixion physiology. Crucifixion would shatter the ulnar nerve that runs through the wrist, causing the fingers to ball up in a condition commonly referred to as 'claw hand'. Jesus' hands really would be like a lion's paw and claw.

Next, we read: 'I can count all my bones, they look and stare at me', **Psalm22:17a**.

We have already noted how crucifixion exaggerates the visibility of the skeletal frame, and Luke completes the picture, telling us:

> And the people stood by looking on. **Luke 23:35a**

 Likewise, the next verse is fulfilled quite literally in the Gospels:

> They divide my garments among them, and for my clothing they cast lots. **Psalm 22:18**

> Then the soldiers . . . took His garments and made four parts, to each soldier a part . . . Now the coat was without seam, woven from the top throughout. Then they said to one another, 'Let's not tear it, but cast lots for it . . .' **John 19:23–24**

**Psalm 22** now returns to those bulls, lions and dogs: 'Save my life from the claw of the dog, rescue me from the mouth of the lion and the horns of the wild ox', **Psalm 22:20–21**.

I can't help noting that:

  – Claws will stripe and slice the flesh, Jesus was whipped, **Matthew 27:26**

- The mouth will crush and maul the flesh, Jesus was beaten, **Matthew 26:67**, **Mark 14:65**, **John 19:3**

- Horns will pierce the flesh, Jesus was pierced by both nails, spear and thorns, **John 19:34**

 **Verse 22** is quoted in the book of **Hebrews** as a general image of Jesus relating to the Church.

> I will talk about your name to my brothers. In the midst of the congregation I will sing your praise. **Hebrews 2:12** (quoting **Psalm 22:22**)

But it is more specifically fulfilled in Jesus' conversation with those crucified with Him. In the midst of the gathered crowd one of the criminals said to Jesus, 'Lord, remember me when you come into your Kingdom', **Luke 23:42**.

The **Psalm** tells us that '. . . when he cried to him, he heard', **Psalm 22:24c**. And Jesus responds '. . . truthfully, today you will be with Me in paradise', **Luke 23:43**. These words are beautifully anticipated in the **Psalm**:

> The humble shall eat and be satisfied. Those who seek after him shall praise *YHWH*. Your heart lives forever. **Psalm 22:26**

Finally, **verses 27 to 31** form a postscript looking back on events. The penultimate verse says, 'A generation will serve Him, it will be told of *YHWH* to the coming generation', **Psalm 22:30**.

This people yet to be born will be told, '. . . that he has done it', **Psalm 22:31b**. Or as the Gospels put it: 'It is finished', **John 19:30**, Jesus' final words from the Cross . . .

. . . although Luke doesn't record this final phrase, he gives us Jesus' penultimate words, which are a quote from the next *Ecstatic Psalm* we are going look at.

## Psalm 31 - Into Your Hands I Commit My Spirit

> Jesus, crying with a loud voice, said, 'Father, into your hands I commit my spirit!' Having said this, He breathed his last. **Luke 23:46**

With His strength failing, Jesus lifts Himself to express an entire inner journey's worth of information in a single breath, this time quoting **Psalm 31**.

**Psalm 22** mirrored the physical events of the Cross while **Psalm 31** tells us about Jesus' inner, emotional journey. It was a pre-prepared sermon delivered in a single phrase. Jesus wanted us to understand that He never lost faith in His Father.

**Psalm 31** starts with an affirmation of faith and a request for help:

> *YHWH*, I have taken refuge in you . . . deliver me

. . . rescue me quickly . . . be a rock of strength
. . . save me! . . . you are my rock and refuge . . .
you lead and guide me . . . you are my strength!
**Psalm 31:1–4**

 **Verse 5** gives Jesus His quote: 'Into your hands I commit my Spirit. You have redeemed me faithful *YHWH Elohim*', **Psalm 31:5**.

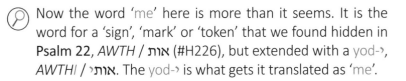 Now the word 'me' here is more than it seems. It is the word for a 'sign', 'mark' or 'token' that we found hidden in **Psalm 22**, *AWTH* / אות (#H226), but extended with a yod-י, *AWTHI* / אותי. The yod-י is what gets it translated as 'me'.

Adding a yod-י to a noun is how Hebrew indicates that something is 'mine'. 'My Son' in **Psalm 2** is the word for a son plus a yod-י, *BNI* / בני. Now the original paleo-Hebrew pictogram for the letter yod-י was an arm and hand, ﺑ. In the logic of Ancient Hebrew something belonged to me because it was 'in-my-hand'.

So, *AWTHI* / אותי / ﺑ+𐤕𐤏 is literally 'sign-of-me' or 'my-token' or even the 'mark-in-my-hand'.

The imagery of these words is remarkable. We can read them in various ways:

- you have redeemed my-token faithful *YHWH Elohim*

- you have redeemed the-mark-in-my-hand faithful *YHWH Elohim*

– you have redeemed my-biggest-sacrifice-fixed-to-a-cross faithful *YHWH Elohim* (see **Psalm 22**)

Whichever way we read this verse, we can see that it is more than just a person being redeemed, something is happening that has contractual implications!

Whether Jesus knew this when He quoted **Psalm 31** is not the issue, God-the-Holy-Spirit knew it when He inspired it, and God-the-Father knew it was there to be discovered and shared by future generations.

But Jesus did know the words of **Psalm 31**. By quoting it He made Himself the speaker expressing His faith through it: 'I trust in *YHWH*. I will rejoice and be glad in your kindness . . .', despite the contradiction of His circumstance: 'You have seen my affliction . . . known the troubles of my soul, but you have not locked me in the hands of the enemy', **Psalm 31:7–8a**.

Notice the 'in-hand' motif: 'Into your hand [God's] . . . you redeemed the mark-in-my-hand . . . you have not locked me in the hands of the enemy!'

The next phrase is remarkable: 'You have set my feet in a wide space', **Psalm 31:8b**. Jesus expresses spiritual freedom while His feet are physically fixed to a thin upright pole.

 **Verses 9 to 13** should be read as descriptive of Jesus' experience on the Cross. They finish by adding a purpose to the conspiracy against Jesus that we first met in **Psalm 2**:

> . . . they took counsel together against me, they schemed to take away my life. **Psalm 31:13**

Matthew, who has previously referenced the counselling together of **Psalm 2** in **Matthew 22:34**, also references **Psalm 31**:

> They took counsel together that they might take Jesus by deceit, and kill him. **Matthew 26:4**

**Verses 14 to 21** fit beautifully into Jesus' mouth on the Cross even though they pre-date Him by a thousand years. They are an affirmation of faith through **prayer**. Then there is a startling revelation:

> . . . I said in my alarm, 'I am cut off from before your eyes', but you heard the sound of my sincere prayer in my cry to you. **Psalm 31:22**

Jesus had asked a question from the Cross, 'my God, my God why have you forsaken me?' **Matthew 27:46**, but this was the sound of a sincere prayer as He passed through despair, it was not the conclusion of a bitter plaintiff.

Like Job, Jesus won a heart victory. In His pain He resisted the temptation to 'curse God and die', **Job 2:9**, expressing instead faith in the face of facts!

 Jesus quotes two **Psalms** from the Cross. Between them, **Psalm 22** and **Psalm 31** take us through the physical and emotional struggle of Jesus' victory, from desperate pain and rejection to faithful confidence that *YHWH*'s goodness is more certain than all injustice.

**Psalm 31** ends with an encouragement for us all.

> Be strong, and let your heart take courage, all you who hope in *YHWH*. **Psalm 31:24**

# Psalm 69 - Vinegar to Drink

**Psalm 69** is an *Ecstatic Psalm*, with predictive elements that cover the whole of Jesus' ministry. It starts:

> Save me *Elohim*, the waters overcome my soul. I sink in the sediment of the deep place, there is no foothold. I have come into deep waters and the currents overwhelm me! **Psalm 69:1b**

Drowning in a stormy ocean was an ancient metaphor for the struggle against chaos, evil and ultimately death. The source of this turmoil is people who 'hate me without cause', **Psalm 69:4**, an idea we also find in **Psalm 35:19** and **Psalm 109:3**. Jesus experienced the same illogical hate and quotes these **Psalms** in **John 15:25**.

In **Psalm 69**, the next line is, '. . . what I did not steal, I have to restore', **Psalm 69:4b**. Like the psalmist, Jesus had to settle a debt that He had not incurred (see **Romans 5:19, 1 Corinthians 6:20, Ephesians 1:7, Colossians 2:14, 1 Peter 2:24**). Then four verses later we read:

I have become estranged from my brothers, an alien to my mother's children, zeal for your house consumes me. **Psalm 69:8–9**

 **Verse 9** is attached to the beginning of Jesus' public ministry, **John 2:17**. Jesus turns over the money tables and is forcibly ejected from the Temple. Jesus is estranged from his 'brothers' in the general sense of countrymen. But 'my mother's children' anticipates sibling disapproval and rejection too, something that we also read about in the Gospels, **Mark 3:21**, **Luke 8:19–21**.

This family tension may have started with this Passover incident, Jesus' zeal may have upset what should have been a family occasion. Certainly John who wrote the Gospel saw it that way, and John is probably Jesus' cousin.

Jesus ends His ministry by cleansing the Temple for a second time. This time it leads to His death at the hands of His countrymen, an event that both His familial brothers and most of His spiritual brethren are absent from too. **Verses 10 to 20** can be read as the inner prayers of Jesus on the Cross. They conclude: 'I looked . . . for comforters, but I found none', **Psalm 69:20**.

 Then we read, 'They also gave me gall for my food. In my thirst, they gave me vinegar to drink', **Psalm 69:21**.

 As Jesus was nailed to the Cross, we read, 'They gave Him sour wine to drink mixed with gall. When He had tasted it, He would not drink', **Matthew 27:34**. But later, 'one of them ran, and took a sponge, and filled it with vinegar, and put it on a reed, and gave Him a drink', **Matthew 27:48**.

It is part of the nature of ecstatic prophecy that it ebbs and flows between the experience of the prophet and the experience of the Cross, and certainly **Psalm 69:22–28** feels more in keeping with David the prototype Messiah than with Jesus who prayed 'Father forgive them . . .' as He was crucified.

Then at the end of the **Psalm** we find David subconsciously expressing faith in Jesus, 'While I am afflicted and in pain, Your Jesus [salvation], *Elohim*, will lift me to safety', **Psalm 69:29b**.

Some translations make this verse a request, but it is a simple declaration of faith. David continues to describe the event he has glimpsed through his own suffering:

> . . . It will please *YHWH* better than an ox, or a bull . . . The humble have seen it, and are glad. You who seek after *Elohim*, let your heart live. **Psalm 69:30–32**

What David has seen is better than any animal sacrifice, it is something the humble can see and find life in!

The **Psalm** ends, 'and those who love his name will dwell in it', **Psalm 69:36b**.

Or as Jesus puts it: 'If a man loves me, he will keep my word. My Father will love him, and we will come to him, and make our dwelling with him', **John 14:23**.

 This is a good point to transfer some notes into your Bible

# Formative Prophecy

Most read Scripture for guidance as well as information. This was true for Jesus too as He grew in 'wisdom, character and favour', **Luke 2:52**.

We have already seen how **Psalm 2**, encouraged 'My Son' to receive the nations by asking the Father for them, **Psalm 2:8**, just days before the devil tried to trade them for worship.

In this section, we will look at other **Psalms** that matched Jesus' circumstance and then offered Him wisdom or encouragement.

## Psalm 91 – The Dove and the Serpent . . .

**Psalm 91** must have been evoked in Jesus' mind by the events of His Baptism. It reads:

He will cover you with his feathers, under his wings you may seek refuge . . . **Psalm 91:4**

And as Jesus came up out of the water, a dove alighted on Him covering Him with its wings and feathers. The words of **Psalm 91** would have followed Jesus into the wilderness where the adversary, Satan, challenged Jesus to presume on its promises.

 He whisked Jesus, either in thought or body, to the pinnacle of the Temple and quotes from **Psalm 91**:

Throw yourself down . . . it is written 'He will put his angels in charge of you . . . and, on their hands they will bear you up, so that you don't dash your foot against a stone'. **Matthew 4:5** and **Luke 4:9** (quoting **Psalm 91:11–12**)

Now it is interesting to note that the word for the 'wing', *kanaph* / כנף (#H3671) that covered Jesus is also the Hebrew word for 'pinnacle', the place where the adversary issues his challenge.

Satan tempts Jesus to presume on the protection promised in the **Psalm**. A floating Messiah in the public square would certainly get Jesus noticed, but the declaration over Jesus as the dove descended referred to the Suffering Servant of Isaiah's prophecies. And the Messiah, '. . . in whom I am well pleased, I have put my Spirit on him . . . he will not shout frenetically to self-promote to get heard in the street', **Isaiah 42:1–3**.

So Satan leaves defeated, and in **Psalm 91** we read: 'You will tread on the lion and the serpent . . . You will trample the young lion and the serpent underfoot.' On the Cross, Jesus would fulfil the Bible's first prophecy as the seed of a woman who crushes the serpent's head as it bit his heel, **Genesis 3:15**. Here at their first encounter, Jesus still treads on 'the old serpent who is called the devil', **Revelation 12:9**, and who is elsewhere called a lion, **1 Peter 5:8**.

Months later in Nazareth the people try to push Jesus over a cliff. Jesus walks safely and supernaturally through the crowd. **Psalm 91** held a promise to draw on when needed but not to be presumed on for glory.

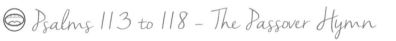

# Psalms 113 to 118 – The Passover Hymn

**Psalms 113 to 118** have been sung at the Passover meal for over 2000 years. They are collectively called the *Hallel,* they were the last act of the Last Supper. Jesus and His disciples, 'after singing a hymn . . . went out to the Mount of Olives', **Matthew 26:30**, **Mark 14:26**.

The *Hallel* weaves praise for God (**Psalms 113**, **115** and **117**) with memories of the Exodus (**Psalms 114** and **116**) into hope for the future (**Psalm 118**). Just hours later, after His arrest, Jesus would have drawn courage from the *Hallel*, particularly from the Exodus **Psalms**.

The cords of death surrounded me, the pains

of Sheol got a hold of me. I found trouble and sorrow. Then I called on the name of *YHWH*: '*YHWH*, I beg you, deliver my life' . . . He [*YHWH*] saved me . . . I shall walk before *YHWH* in the land of the living. **Psalm 116:3–4,6,9**

# Psalm 116 – The Cup of Jesus

**Psalm 116** includes the line, 'I shall lift up the cup of salvation'. 'Salvation' is the name Jesus / ישוע extended with a wav-ו and a tav-ת, a peg-ץ and a cross-✝.

The 'cup of Jesus-fixed-to-a-cross' was an important part of Passover. Four times during the meal diners drank from a cup or cups to remember the four promises made to Israel at the first Passover: 'I will bring you out of Egypt', *sanctification*; 'I will deliver you', *deliverance*; 'I will redeem you', *redemption*; and 'I will take you for My people', *restoration* (see **Exodus 6:6–7**).

In Gethsemane Jesus prays, 'Let this cup pass from Me, though not My will, but Yours', **Matthew 26:39**.

Jesus was about to seal a new deal with His 'blood of the Covenant'. He had appropriated the cup which carried His name and the Passover promises. But in the Garden the cost of fulfilling this pledge weighed heavy. However **Psalm 116** proceeds, 'I will fulfil my promise to *YHWH* in the presence of all his people', **Psalm 116:14**.

Now this verse could be translated: 'I will fulfil my promise to *YHWH* entreating for all his people'. The difference comes down to how you translate the compound word *na-ngdh* / נגדה-נא.

*Ngdh* / נגדה (#H5048) means to 'stand before', or 'to give an account before'. It is joined to the particle *na* / נא (#H4994) which can make an action a plea or an entreaty, or simply give immediacy to an action. The difference is seen in **Genesis 18:4** which the NASB translates '*Please* let a little water be bought . . .' but which the World English Bible makes '*Now* let a little water be fetched . . .'

So, *na-ngdh* / נגדה-נא can be an immediate-standing-in-front-of, 'in the presence of' or it can mean standing-up-to-plead, 'entreating'. Both are true of Jesus' sacrifice; it was public, and it was intercession for the world!

 Then we read: 'Precious in the sight of *YHWH* is the death of his holy ones . . . I am your servant . . .', **Psalm 116:15–16a**.

There is a fascinating resonance between the themes I've just colour-coded above, the Last Supper and Isaiah's Suffering Servant, of whom we read:

> My servant . . . he poured out himself out to death, and was numbered with the law-breakers; yet he bore the sin of many, and interceded [entreated] for the law-breakers. **Isaiah 53:12**

At the Last Supper:

> He [Jesus] gave it [the cup] to them saying, '. . .
> this is my blood of the promise which is poured
> out for many for the forgiveness of sins . . .' And
> after singing a **Hymn [Psalm 116]** they went out
> . . . **Matthew 26:28–30**

(The Servant/Jesus; The poured out cup; Intercession for
forgiveness of sins; All the many people; and Promise
sealed by blood/death)

In Gethsemane, Jesus prayed for the cup to pass from
Him, but kept His vow to the Father.

But the ***Passover Hymn***, the *Hallel*, is not finished, **Psalm
118** has something to say too.

# Psalm 118 – The Rejected Cornerstone

**Psalm 118** contains one of the New Testament's favourite
Old Testament quotes.

'The stone which the builders rejected has become the
head of the corner. This is *YHWH*'s doing. It is marvellous
in our eyes', **Psalm 118:22–23**, is quoted in **Matthew
21:42–46**, **Mark 12:10–11** and **Luke 20:17** as Jesus taught
on the day before the Last Supper.

He uses it to conclude the parable in which some vine-growers kill the vineyard owner's son and the vineyard is given to new tenants.

Jesus explains that spiritual authority was being taken from the priests to be given to a new community. This truth was illustrated just weeks later when Peter was arrested for preaching this same verse in the Temple, **Acts 4:11**.

Peter presents Jesus as the rejected stone, but Jesus had given Simon the name 'Peter', which meant 'rock' too, **Matthew 16:18**. So by his first letter, Peter saw Christ becoming a new priestly community of living stones through Him (again quoting **Psalm 118**).

> You also, as living stones, are built up as a spiritual house, to be a holy priesthood . . . So, this is precious for you who believe, but for those who are disobedient, 'The stone which the builders rejected, has become the chief cornerstone,' . . . But you are a chosen race, a royal priesthood, a holy community . . . **1 Peter 2:8–9**

This verse was important to the young Church. They were not simply a new synagogue within the old system, they were a brand new spiritual administration. Paul teaches the same in **Ephesians 2:20–22**.

Now **Psalm 118** is primarily formative, it encouraged Jesus as He fulfilled Passover. As He sang it at the Last Supper He would have noticed **verse 22**, 'Blessed is the one who comes in the name of the Lord', because these words had been sung to Him as He rode into Jerusalem at the start of the week.

And three times the **Psalm** uses the Jesus' name in its more formal spelling *Yshuah* / ישועה (see **verses 14,15 and 21**).

These points of connection may have caught Jesus' attention. Its words would have encouraged Him in His final hours:

> In distress, I called on *Yah*; *Yah* answered me in a wide space. The Lord is for me . . . what can man do? . . . I shall not die, but live . . . *YHWH* . . . has not given me over to death. **Psalm 118:5–6, 17–18**

And as Jesus was nailed to the Cross, He would understand how the words, 'fasten the festival sacrifice with bands to the horns (things-that-stick-out, see **Psalm 22**) of the altar', **Psalm 118:27**, were about Him and so the **Psalm** was for Him.

> *Yah*, my strength and **song** is **for** me, **for** **Jesus**[salvation] . . . *I shall not die but live* . . . **Psalm 118:14–17**

**Psalm 118** may not be 'of David', but it is 'for the Beloved'.

We looked at the Psalms with a lot of prophetic content, but there are lots more prophetic lines and verses in the Psalms. You may want read and add notes to the verses listed on the next two pages. So...

 . . . this is a good point to transfer some notes into your Bible

*Some more Prophecies from the* **Psalms** *to highlight in your Bible:*

Psalm 16:10 – see **Matthew 7:14**

Psalm 34:20 – 'He keeps all his bones, not one of them is broken' fulfilled by Jesus, **John 19:33,36**.

Psalm 35:9 – 'My soul shall be joyful in the LORD. It shall rejoice in his salvation'. Quoted by Mary in the song she composes while pregnant with Jesus, **Luke 1:46–47**. It contains Jesus' name in the word 'salvation'.

It also contains a run of predictive verses.

35:11 – Malicious witnesses rise up, they ask me things that I do not know.

For many gave false testimony against him . . . and some stood up and gave false testimony . . . **Mark 14:56–57**

35:12a – They repay me evil for good.

Jesus answered them, 'I have shown you many good works from my Father. For which of those works do you stone me?' **John 10:32**

35:15b – The smiters whom I did not know gathered together against me.

Having blindfolded Him, they struck Him on the face and asked him, 'Prophesy! Who is the one who struck you?' **Luke 22:64**

Psalm 38:10–12 – '. . . My heart throbs, my strength fails me. My loved ones and my friends stand aloof from my assault, and my acquaintances stand far off . . .' On the Cross, Jesus is abandoned by all His disciples bar John, but other acquaintances do stand at a distance, **Luke 23:49**.

Psalm 42:9 – 'I will say to God my rock, "why have you forgotten me?"' We often miss this reference to Jesus' experience of separation from His Father because **Psalm22** says it so much more clearly.

Psalm 55:12–15 – See Judas.

Psalm 68:18 – 'You have ascended on high, you have led away captives and have received gifts among men . . .' This verse is quoted by Paul, **Ephesians 4:8**, but we miss the reason why it is so clearly related to Jesus. The next verse reads 'Blessed be my Lord who daily bears our burdens, The God who is our Jesus [salvation]!'

Psalm 80:8 – 'You removed a vine from Egypt'. This verse relates to Jesus' childhood experience. **Psalm 80:8–19** refers to events in Israel's past but the Hebrew is written in the imperfect state, as if events are not yet completed. Matthew sees them fulfilled in Jesus, **Matthew 2:15**. Note how the vine is referred to as a 'son' (verse 15) and as the 'son of man' (**verse 17**).

Psalm 89:3–4,29,36 – See **Luke 1:33**

# Part 3

## Types & Titles, Teaching & the Trinity

# Types & Titles

David is a 'type' of Christ, so we have already seen Jesus by type in the *Messianic Psalms*. But **Psalms** contains other typological images too. There is the High Priest, whose role is modelled in the three verses of **Psalm 133**:

1  The High Priest (Aaron) joins (Levi) people together

2  . . . by sharing his anointing with those in worship (Zion) . . .

3  . . . and connecting them to blessing and eternal life

The book of **Hebrews** presents Jesus as the substance which this role foreshadowed (see **Hebrews 3:1**, **4:14** etc).

Similarly, we see the God / Good Shepherd in a number of **Psalms** (see **Psalm 28:9**, **Psalm 78:72**) but most beautifully in **Psalm 23**.

## Psalm 23 – He will be My Shepherd

**Psalm 23** is a favourite the world over. Its opening line (after the title and credits) is 'The Lord is my Shepherd' from which we get the Divine title *YHWH Rohi* / רעי יהוה.

YHWH, the covenantal name of God, is related to the verb for being, אהיה / 'I am' or יהיה / 'He will be'. *YHWH* is the living-promise of the phrase it is joined to!

So *YHWH Rohi*, promises 'I am / He will be my shepherd'. It is fulfilled in Jesus: 'I AM the good Shepherd', **John 10:14**.

 Interestingly, **Psalm 23** is an exposition of the other eight *YHWH* promises, all of which are fulfilled by Jesus. The ultimate cryptic typological prophecy! Let's look at it line by line.

## Psalm 23: A Psalm of David

| YHWH Rohi / YHWH my Shepherd | 'I am the Good Shepherd.' John 10:11,14 |
|---|---|
| [1]*YHWH* is my shepherd, I shall not lack. | The **Psalm** is an exposition of the good shepherd's care. It demonstrates that the shepherd knows his sheep's needs and describes how the sheep know him. |
| YHWH Yireh / YHWH will provide, or YHWH will see to it | Spoken prophetically by Abraham as he looks into the distance for a substitute sacrifice in the very location where Jesus would be crucified. **Genesis 22:8** |
| [2]He makes me lie down in green pastures, | Jesus fulfils this promise and says, 'Abraham rejoiced to see my day, he saw it and was glad.' **John 8:56** |

| | |
|---|---|
| ***YHWH Shalom /*** **YHWH is** Peace **(offering)** <br><br> He leads me beside quiet waters, | The name is given through Gideon. He is threshing wheat in a winepress for fear of the Midianites when *YHWH* appears and says '. . . Peace to you.' **Judges 6:23–24** <br><br> Jesus appears to His fear-filled disciples and says '. . . Peace be to you' **John 20:19** <br><br> As Paul puts it, 'We have peace with God through our Lord Jesus Christ.' **Romans 5:1** |
| ***YHWH Rophe /*** **YHWH my** Healer <br><br> [3]He restores my soul. | This name is given when *YHWH* makes the bitter waters at Marah drinkable, **Exodus 15:26**. Although the name is used only once in the Bible, the concept of *YHWH*'s healing and restoration reappears over 60 times through the Old Testament story. <br><br> Of Jesus we read, 'He healed all that were sick.' **Matthew 8:16** |
| ***YHWH Tsidkenu / YHWH* my** Righteousness <br><br> He guides me in the paths of righteousness for his name's sake. | Jeremiah uses this name twice, **Jeremiah 23:6**, **33:16**. Both talk about a quality of YHWH to be revealed at a future time. The first use is tied to the coming of the 'Branch of David', a title for the Messiah. <br><br> The New Testament sees God's people, 'Filled with the fruits of righteousness that come through Jesus Christ', **Philippians 1:11** |

### YHWH Shamah / YHWH is There

⁴Though I walk through the valley of the shadow of death, I will fear no evil for you are with me. Your rod and your staff, they comfort me.

Ezekiel has a vision in which he sees YHWH leave the Temple and Jerusalem, but at the end of his book he 'sees' a new spiritual temple and a city called YHWH Shamah, or YHWH is there. God would be with His people again.

As 'Emmanuel', 'God with us' Jesus fulfills this name, but He also promises: 'Lo I am with you always, even to the end of the age.' **Matthew 28:20**

### YHWH Nissi / YHWH my Banner/(Victory)

⁵You prepare a table before me in the presence of my enemies. You anoint my head with oil. My cup overflows.

This name is used in Exodus as a celebration of Joshua's victory over the Amalekites. The banner is a victory banner and Joshua is a type of Jesus, so the New Testament tells us about,

> God who gives us the victory through Jesus Christ. **1 Corinthians 15:7**

### YHWH Mkedesh / YHWH my Sanctifier

⁶Surely goodness and loving kindness shall follow me all the days of my life . . .

This name is used 7 times in **Leviticus** 20–22, a passage that twice hides a reference to the blood of Jesus, see *Volume 5: Jesus in the Wilderness*. The idea of our sanctification through the sacrifice and blood of Jesus appears throughout the New Testament:

> We have been sanctified through the offering of the body of Jesus Christ. **Hebrews 10:10** (also **Colossians 1:22**)

For however many are the promises of God [*YHWH*], in Him [Jesus] is the 'Yes', so also through Him is the 'Amen'. **2 Corinthians 1:20**

# Psalm 40 – The Servant Sacrifice

**Psalm 40** is a song of gratitude; every word would make sense if sung by Jesus. But I'm giving it space here because the book of **Hebrews** links it to a type, the perfect servant!

> . . . he says: 'Sacrifice and offering you didn't desire, *but you prepared a body for me*; You had no pleasure in whole burnt offerings and sacrifices for sin.' **Hebrews 10:5–6**

But in quoting **Psalm 40**, the writer of **Hebrews** has changed the middle phrase. Instead of '*but you prepared a body for me*', **Psalm 40:6** reads: '*You have pierced my ears*'.

This is not a mistake, it is a Jewish way of teaching; expanding one passage with related information from another. Because piercing an ear meant owning a body!

Israelites could not own slaves, but they could bond their service to each other. Initially this was for seven years during which the Hebrew text tells us: 'he comes in *in-his-body*, he shall leave *in-his-body*', **Exodus 21:3**. The bondsman is giving his body to serve. After seven years the servant could quit or freely choose to serve their master for 'eternity', **Exodus 21:6**. To become a 'forever servant', the volunteer's ear was pierced. A deal was sealed with blood and their body was permanently marked!

The writer of **Hebrews** sees a model of Jesus in this volunteer-slave. They become a living sacrifice by the piercing of their freely gifted body.

This is a good point to transfer some notes into your Bible

# The Trinity & Jesus' Divinity

In *Volume 2: Jesus in the Beginning* we saw how **Psalm 33** was combined with the Creation account to illustrate aspects of *YHWH* that were part of Him but also distinct, 'the Word' and 'the Spirit'. **Psalm 33** is an Old Testament passage that helps us to see the Trinity before we get to the New Testament. In the New Testament Jesus uses **Psalm 82** and **110** to teach His Divinity.

## Psalm 82 – Shared Divinity

In the dying days of 32 AD, after the feast of Dedication, Jesus proclaims: 'I and the Father are one!' **John 10:30**. The

Temple authorities want to stone Jesus who challenges them to explain something from **Psalm 82**.

> . . . Isn't it written in your law, 'I said, you are gods?' If He called them gods, to whom the word of God came (and the Scripture can't be broken), do you say of Him whom the Father sanctified and sent into the world, 'You blaspheme,' because I said, 'I am the Son of God?' **John 10:34–36**

The Temple authorities were Sadducees. Sadducees denied the existence of angels and other spiritual beings, **Acts 23:8**, so when they read the start of **Psalm 82**, 'God [*Elohim*] stands in the congregation of God [*El*] . . .', they were forced to conclude that the congregation was made up of humans not angelic beings.

But God calls the congregation 'gods'! The phrase Jesus quotes is emphatic: 'I, I said, "you are gods"'. God, who can't lie, calls people 'gods', His word makes them Divine. The **Psalm** continues: 'you are all sons of the Most-High', **Psalm 82:6**.

Jesus has led the Sadducees into a paradox of their own design, they can't complain about His claim to be the 'Son of God' when by their own theology they are that and more.

Jesus' use of **Psalm 82** impacts Peter's thinking. If a word from God has the power to impute His nature, then how much more the coming of his Son, The Word. Peter starts his second letter acknowledging Jesus who:

> . . . has granted to us His precious and magnificent promises, in order that we might become partakers in His divine nature . . . **2 Peter 1:3b–4a**

# Psalm 110 – The Divine Priest-King

In the days before His Crucifixion, Jesus asks the Pharisees, '. . . the Messiah, whose Son is He?' **Matthew 22:42**. When they reply 'David's', Jesus quotes **Psalm 110:1** drawing out all three Persons of the Trinity as He does so:

> How does David in the [Holy] Spirit call him 'Lord' saying, 'The Lord [God the Father] said to my Lord [God the Son], sit at My right hand until I make your enemies a footstool. **Matthew 22:43–44**

Father, Son and Holy Spirit are all there in the opening verse of **Psalm 110**. It is the most cited Old Testament verse in the New Testament, with eleven references.

Quoted verbatim: by Jesus in three Gospels (**Matthew 22:44**, **Mark 12:36**, **Luke 20:42–43**); by Peter on the day of Pentecost (**Acts 2:35**); and in Hebrews (**Hebrews 1:13**). And by subject, ie sitting at the right hand of God: once by Jesus at his trial (**Matthew 26:64**); twice by Paul (**Ephesians 1:20** and **Colossians 3:1**); and three times in Hebrews (**Hebrews 1:3c, 8:1b, 10:12**).

The importance of **Psalm 110** to the Christology of the brand-new Church can't be overstated, it is the climax of Peter's sermon on the day of Pentecost. Peter starts in **Psalm 16**. David was 'always seeing *YHWH* . . . ' and says *YHWH* will not allow His 'Holy One to undergo decay', **Psalm 16:8,10**. And Peter ends the first evangelistic sermon in **Psalm 110** where David saw the 'Holy One' now sitting at *YHWH*'s right hand. This vision was of Jesus (see **Acts 2:25–35**).

Peter calls for a response and 3000 people are baptised, fulfilling:

> *YHWH* shall send a *tribe*(rod) out of Zion . . .
> Your people, *willing-volunteers* in the day of your *army*(power), in holy array from the womb of the morning . . . **Psalm 110:2–3**

Note: 'rod', 'sceptre' and 'tribe' are all translations of Hebrew *mattah* / מטה (#H4294), see 'the tribe of Judah', **Numbers 1:27**. The word for 'power', *chayl* / חיל (#H2342), is more properly a means of holding power, a force of 'armed men', see **Deuteronomy 11:4**.

The 3000 *volunteers* of Pentecost become the first wave of the *empowered tribe* that God sends into the world. A tribe that we are also a part of!

In the next verse, the **Psalm** adds a priestly calling for the Divine descendant of David.

> YHWH has sworn and will not change His mind: 'You are a priest forever, of the order of Melchizedek'. **Psalm 110:4**

We explored Melchizedek as a type of Christ in *Volume 3: Jesus in the Fathers*. His name means 'King-of-righteousness' or 'A-just-King'. If we translate it that way, **verse 4** becomes: 'You are a priest forever, a-just-king by My decree.'

During the Intertestamental period, the Rabbis had noticed that the Old Testament expected a priestly Messiah as well as a regal one (the anointed priest from Aaron is covered in more detail in *Volume 5: Jesus in the Wilderness*). There was a contemporary debate about whether these different 'Messiahs' were one or more people. **Psalm 110** draws the anointed roles of priest and king together.

**Hebrews** uses **Psalm 110** to explain Jesus. It specifically links the priestly function of the Messiah to the kingly privilege of sitting at God's right hand.

> We have such a high priest, who sat down on the right hand of the throne of the Majesty in the heavens. **Hebrews 8:1**

> But He, when He had offered one sacrifice for sins forever, sat down on the right hand of God waiting from that time 'until His enemies are made a stool for his feet.' **Hebrews 10:12–13**

**Hebrews** following **Psalm 110** sees Divinity in the Priest-King.

> His Son . . . is the radiance of the glory of God and the exact imprint of his nature . . . and when He had by himself made purification for our sins, He sat down on the right hand of the Majesty on high. **Hebrews 1:3**

## Jesus' Teaching in the Psalms

> Listen my people to my teaching . . . I will open my mouth in a parable (*mashal* / משל) I will utter puzzles (*hidoth* / חידות) of old. **Psalm 78:1–2**

A parable or *mashal* (#H4912) was a simple story that explained a deeper truth. And a *hidoth* (#H2420) was a puzzle that had to be untangled, it comes from a root word that means to 'tie a knot'. Parables and knotty problems, it is the way that Jesus taught:

> I speak to them in parables, because seeing they do not see, and hearing they do not hear, nor do they understand. **Matthew 13:13**

 And a lot of what Jesus taught was from the **Psalms** too. In fact, every one of the beatitudes in Jesus' seminal 'Sermon on the Mount' is found as a seed idea in the **Psalms**.

– Blessed are the poor in Spirit, for theirs is the Kingdom of Heaven.

> The poor man cried, and *YHWH* heard him, and saved him out of all his troubles. **Psalm 34:6**
>
> *YHWH* is near to those who have a broken heart, and saves those who have a crushed spirit. **Psalm 34:18**

– Blessed are those who mourn, for they shall be comforted.

> You have turned for me my mourning into dancing, removed my sackcloth, and clothed me with gladness. **Psalm 30:11**

– Blessed are the gentle, for they shall inherit the earth.

> But the meek shall inherit the land [earth]. **Psalm 37:11**

– Blessed are those who hunger and thirst for righteousness, for they shall be satisfied.

> God, you are my God. I will earnestly seek you, my soul thirsts for you, my flesh longs for you . . . my soul shall be satisfied . . . **Psalm 63:1,5**

– Blessed are the merciful, for they shall receive mercy.

> With the merciful you will show yourself merciful. **Psalm 18:25**

– Blessed are the pure in heart, for they shall see God.

> With the pure, you will show yourself pure. **Psalm 18:26**

He who has clean hands and a pure heart . . . shall receive a blessing from *YHWH* . . . This is the generation of those who seek your face. **Psalm 22:4–6**

– **Blessed are the peacemakers for they shall be called sons of God.**

   . . . seek peace, and pursue it. **Psalm 34:14**

   . . . for there is a future for the man of peace. **Psalm 37:37**

– **Blessed are those who have been persecuted for the sake of righteousness, for theirs is the Kingdom of Heaven**

   Many are the afflictions of the righteous, but *YHWH* delivers him out of them. **Psalm 34:19**

Ultimately Jesus is the great parable, the story that illustrated and untangled something in eternity. God's message doesn't change, but in the light of the Gospel the meaning of Scripture is profoundly shaken up. Jesus is the 'mystery of God . . . in whom all the treasures of wisdom and knowledge are hidden,' **Colossians 2:2–3**.

The list below suggests some other verses you might want to look at. There is far more of Jesus in the **Psalms** than we've had space to cover in this short book!

This is a good point to transfer some notes into your Bible

*Some more Types, Titles and Teaching from the* Psalms *to highlight in your Bible:*

 **Psalm 1:6** compare *YHWH* with Jesus in **John 10:14**

 **Psalm 8:2** quoted by Jesus, **Matthew 11:23, 21:1**

 **Psalm 11:6** explains nature of the cup Jesus takes in our place, **Matthew 20:22**

 **Psalm 19:14** uses the title 'Rock and Redeemer', see **1 Corinthians 10:4, Galatians 3:13, Titus 2:14**

 **Psalm 27:1** uses the title 'Light and Salvation', see **John 8:12, 1 Thessalonians 5:9**

 **Psalm 36:8–9** is background to Jesus' teaching on Water and Light at the Feast of Tabernacles, **John 7:37–8:12**

 **Psalm 43:3** truth, light and the way to the Holy Hill, **John 14:6**

 **Psalm 49:16–20**, the seed to the parable of the Rich Fool, **Luke 12:16–21**

 **Psalm 50:11**, every bird is considered by God, **Matthew 6:26, Luke 12:6**

 **Psalm 68:19** reads literally, 'Blessed is my Lord who daily lifts our burdens, God our Jesus!'

Psalm 72:17 reads literally, 'For as long as the sun shines, his name will endure, his name shall be nun'. The letter 'nun' was also the number 14 and is a cryptic title. See **Matthew 1:17** and *Volume 6: Jesus in War and Peace*

Psalm 80 uses three titles that Jesus applies to Himself. **Verse 1**, 'The Shepherd' see **John 10:11**; **verse 8**, 'The vine' see **John 15:1**, 'brought out of Egypt' see **Matthew 2:19–20**; **verse 17**, 'The son of man'

Psalm 97:7 assigned to Jesus in **Hebrews 1:6**, fulfilled in **Luke 2:13–14**

Psalm 103:2–5 *YHWH*'s benefits seen in Jesus, see **Matthew 9:6, Luke 9:11, Galatians 3:13**

Psalm 146:6 is quoted in **Acts 4:24**. **Verses 7 and 8** describe the context of **Acts 4**: Justice for the oppressed, **Acts 4:17,21**; food for the hungry, **Acts 4:34**; prisoners set free, **Acts 4:13**; raising up the bowed down, **Acts 3:8**

The name Jesus / ישוע (#H3444) appears in the following thirty-three **Psalms**: 3:8, 9:14, 13:5, 14:7, 18:50, 20:5, 21:1, 22:1, 28:8, 35:3 & 9, 42:5&11, 43:5, 44:4, 53:6, 62:1–2&6, 67:2, 68:19, 69:29, 70:4, 74:12, 78:22, 80:2, 88:1, 89:26, 91:16, 96:2, 98:2–3, 106:4, 116:13, 118:14–5&21, 119:123 & 155 & 166 & 174, 140:7, 149:4

# Summary

In the Psalms we have seen Jesus revealed in many ways:

 We have seen the Psalms prophesy every major development and phase of Jesus' life. From womb (**Psalm 18**), through tomb to eternity and more (**Psalm 45**).

 They have added understanding to models of Christ like the perfect Servant, the Good Shepherd, the Bridegroom and the Messiah.

 From 'Blessed are the meek' (**Psalm 37**) to 'into your hands I commit my Spirit' (**Psalm 31**) Jesus uses the **Psalms** as both foundation and flair in His own teaching . . .

 . . . So we have read words that spoke to Jesus' Mother and were about His brothers (**Psalm 69**), many that were written by His forbear David . . .

 . . . who left a testimony to Jesus' Divinity (**Psalm 110**).

 But it was the Korahites who foresaw the ultimate appearance of God in the flesh (**Psalm 84**).

 We've untangled knotty problems that hid Jesus in the Hebrew (**Psalms 22**) or tangled Him up with His close-knit friends (**Psalm 41**).

But there is more to find than we've covered in these pages. That's part of your job! The Jesus Centred Bible project is constantly evolving – please get in contact through *jesuscentred.org* and join in the discussion.

. . . this brings us to the end of our look at the Psalms. We will pick up the story of Jesus in the Old Testament in the next volume:

# 11
# Jesus in the
# Major Prophets

*Incarnation, Crucifixion, Resurrection & Ascension*

## Isaiah – Daniel

# Appendix – Psalm Index

# Jesus in the Old Testament Series (proposed plan)

 **Jesus in the Old Testament:** OUT NOW
*An introduction*
Genesis – Malachi
978-0-9933445-1-0

 **Jesus in the Beginning:**
*Creation & Primeval History*
Genesis 1 – 12  OUT
978-0-9933445-5-8  NOW

 **Jesus in the Fathers:**
*Patriarchs & Promises*
Genesis 12 – 50  OUT
978-0-9933445-7-2  NOW

 **Jesus in the Great Escape:** SUMMER 2018
*Out of Egypt*
Exodus
978-0-9933445-5-8

 **Jesus in the Wilderness:**
*Signs and Wanders*
Leviticus – Deuteronomy
978-0-9933445-8-9

 **Jesus in War and Peace:**
*The Age of Heroes and Heroines*
Joshua – Ruth

 **Jesus in the United Nation:**
*Under an anointed Prophet, Priest and King*
1 &2 Samuel – 1 Kings

 **Jesus in Division and Defeat:**
*Prophetic Purpose in a Broken People*
2 Kings – 1 & 2 Chronicles

 **Jesus in Words of Wisdom:**
*For Life, Love and Loss*
Job – Song of Songs

 **Jesus in Worship and Wonder:** THIS BOOK!
*Melody, Mystery and the Messiah*  Psalms
978-0-9933445-9-6

 **Jesus in the Major Prophets:**
*Incarnation, Crucifixion, Resurrection and Ascension*
Isaiah – Daniel

 **Jesus in the Minor Prophets:**
*Revealing the Plans of God*
Hosea – Malachi

 **Jesus in Exile and Return:**
*Creating a Space for Grace*
Ezra – Esther + input from the prophets

 **Jesus in the Silent Years:**
*Providence in the Wait for The Messiah*
End of the Old Testament to start of the Gospels